# COMBAT MACHETE
## VOLUME ONE: FUNDAMENTALS

BY
JOSEPH TRUNCALE & FERNAN VARGAS

PRO-SYSTEMS / BUSHI SATORI RYU

COMBAT MACHETE VOLUME ONE

BY

Joseph J. Truncale and Fernan Vargas

**PHOTO MODELS:**
Anthony Calderone, Joseph Truncale, & Fernan Vargas

# www.RavenTactical.com

# COMBAT MACHETE

# VOLUME ONE

## Copyright© 2017

The authors and publishers of this manual accept no liability whatsoever for any injuries to persons or property resulting from applications or adoption of any of these procedures, considerations or tactics presented or implied in this text. This training manual in not designed or intended to function as a self-teaching manual of techniques. This course is to be taught by a certified instructor and the manual is only a training aid used for reference. No part of this book may be reproduced in any form or by any means without permission, in writing from Raven Tactical International or the Authors.

**First Printing 2017**
**Raven Tactical International**
Chicago, Illinois USA
www.RavenTactical.com

# TABLE OF CONTENTS

| | |
|---|---|
| Introduction: A brief history of the Machete | 55 |
| Safety In Training | 13 |
| Use of Force | 16 |
| Nomenclature | 22 |
| Methods of Carry | 24 |
| Uses of the Machete | 26 |
| Target Selection | 29 |
| Stance, balance and movement | 33 |
| Basic gripping techniques | 37 |
| Defensive Techniques | 41 |
| Slashing techniques | 47 |
| Thrusting techniques | 59 |
| Machete Drills | 64 |
| Combat Techniques | 72 |
| Multiple Attackers | 76 |
| Warrior mind-set principles | 79 |
| References and suggested material | 84 |
| About the authors | 87 |
| Books by the authors | 94 |
| Special thanks | |

# INTRODUCTION: BRIEF HISTORY OF THE MACHETE

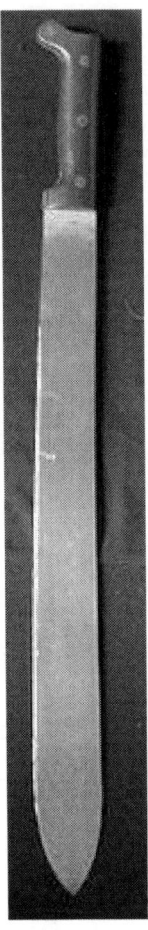

The machete is a combination of a large knife, axe and a short sword and the practicality of this tool has made it popular all over the world. The term machete comes from the Spanish language and the first part of the name (Macho) means male or strong and used to refer to sledgehammers. There are numerous variations of the same tool depending on the specific area or country. The machete is popular all over South America, and also in places like Guyana, Barbados Grenada, Jamaica, Tobago and other countries.

The machete is often used to cut through thick brush as well as for doing various jobs in agricultural communities. The machete is also used as a favorite weapon of many countries and has been used in numerous battles all over the world. It is a weapon used by many ethnic groups in West Africa. In the Philippines they also use a machete like tool called a "bolo" which is employed for chopping through the jungle and for combat. The Filipino art of "Arnis" (Eskrima) is a fighting system which employees both the stick and the knife or short sword (Bolo) in their system

Another popular machete is the "Kukri" which has a slightly curved blade which is used by the Nepalese. In fact, the Nepalese soldiers carry a Kukri machete as part of their equipment. China also has a tool they use (DAO) for practical uses and for combat. In many countries the machete is carried on their person and used for practical jobs and for combat and fighting. Even Russia has their version of the machete called a "Taiga." In fact, they also have their armed services, including their Special Forces carry a Taiga. The Japanese "Wakizashi" which is a short sword is similar to a machete in the length and having a sharp edge and an unsharpened side. Most of the techniques of using the "Wakizashi" are similar or the same as the machete combat techniques.

Colombia is the largest exporter of machetes in the world.

Interestingly, there is even a country's flag (Angola) that shows a machete as part of the design. The Bolo machete and the Gerber machete /saw combination are also popular in Latin and North America.

Throughout countries in Africa, Southeast Asia, Latin America and the Caribbean the machete has been the weapon of choice of agricultural workers and guerilla fighters alike. Machetes have been used with great efficiency in rebel uprisings, revolts and guerilla actions in countries such as Brazil, Cuba, The Dominican Republic, the Philippines, and Kenya. In countries such as Rwanda and Haiti, the Machete has a much more sinister history, being closely associated with human relights violations and even attempts at genocide. The machete also finds itself at the side of soldiers across the globe, as part of their general issue equipment.

In the larger cultural scope the machete has a role in cultural identity of laborers around the world. In Brazil and islands in the Caribbean such as Cuba, Puerto Rico and Haiti the machete has plays a role in folkloric dance and games.

As a formal fighting art the Machete is taught in martial traditions such as, Mani, Capoeria, Kali, Silat, Guazabara, and Colombian esgrima de machete. Similar weapons are taught in various forms of Kung Fu, Krabi Krabong and historical western fencing arts.

The Machete has also found its way into the hands of criminals. It is a signature weapon of M6-13 the notorious gang springing from El Salvador, and is used by gangs and cartels throughout North and South America World wide crime statistics identify the machete as the number one edged weapon used in assaults.

## A BOLO MACHETE

## GERBER MACHETE/SAW COMBO

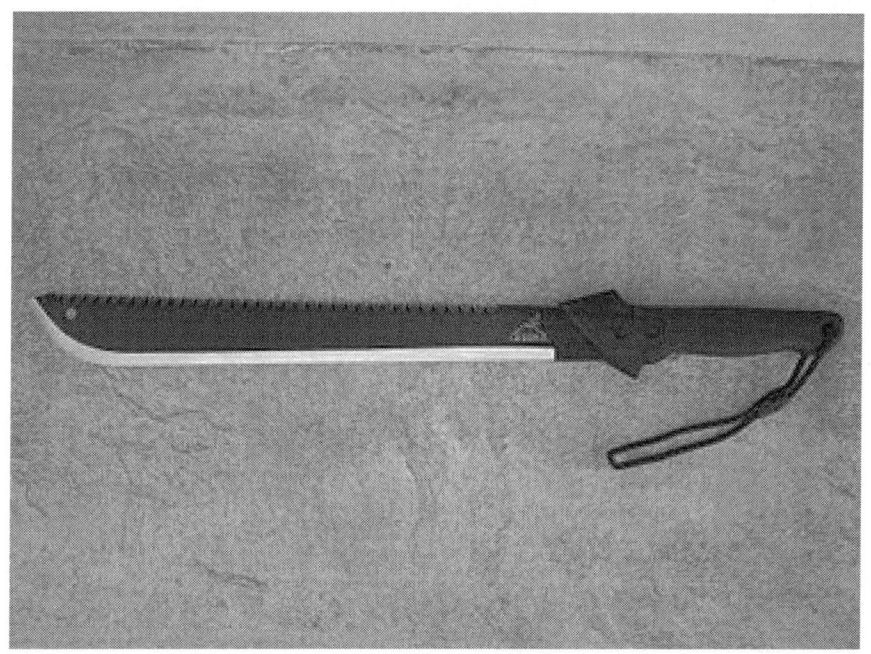

# U.S. MILITARY MACHETE HISTORY

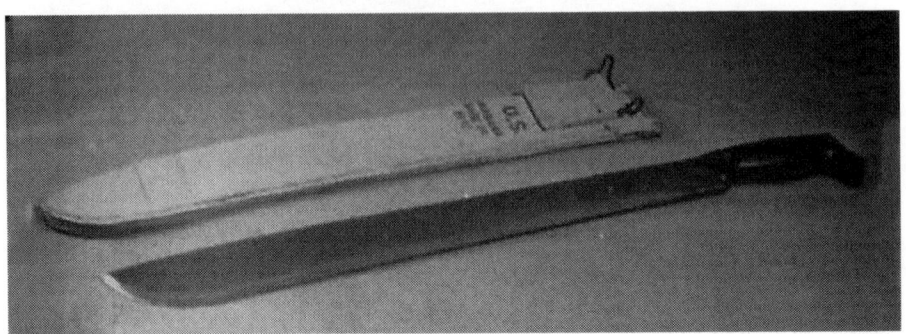

*M-1942 machete and canvas duck sheath, with M1910 hook. World War II QMG photo.*

"Prior to World War II a 22 inch machete was in use by the Army, but trials in Panama showed that a shorter design was better. The machete adopted as the M-1942 was an 18-inch straight back modification of the Collins commercial type, proved by extensive use in the tropics."

This was the basic tool of jungle operations, permitting travel through the tangled vegetation away from the trails. The machete depended on velocity rather than weight for its cutting action, being allowed to pivot in the hand with the stroke, while held only with the thumb, index and middle fingers. A hole was drilled in the handle for a wrist cord, which kept the machete from being dropped or lost. The machete was also considered a decidedly useful weapon, especially for the silent disposition of sentries and in night ambushes. (Photo to the left shows 101st airborne soldiers with a Nazi flag captured in a village assault near Utah Beach, St. Marcouf, France, 8 June 1944. Right paratrooper is holding a machete that seems to have a bright finish.)

The sheath was made of heavy, water-repellent duck, which resisted the mildew and dampness that destroyed leather in the jungle. A brass top and staples prevented the sheath from being cut by the blade. A hook (M-1910 type) was provided to attach the machete to a pack or to the pistol or cartridge belt. The machete dimensions were about 22 1/2" overall with a 17 7/8" blade that was 2" wide.

Most World War II machetes had black plastic grips, but True Temper machetes stamped 1945 were made with olive green plastic handles. Other machetes were made for the U.S. military in the World War II period. A U.S. Navy Mk1 model had a 26 inch blade and some of the older, 28 inch or longer machetes remained in service. There was a paratrooper machete with a 16 inch packetized blade, 22 inches overall. A folding machete was also issued to some units.

The machete itself has changed little since World War II, but the scabbard (or sheath) has evolved through several models. The earliest sheaths were a plain canvas stock with a belt loop. The M-1942 machete had a sturdy canvas duck scabbard with the M-1910 belt hook. The last WW II model had a smooth, hard OD plastic case with a metal throat similar to a bayonet. That last style was in use until the Vietnam War, approximately 1966. In 1967 a new style carrier was issued that is very similar to today's machete sheath.

The current version of the machete sheath (photo, below) differs only in color from the Vietnam era M-1967 issue scabbard. The NSN has changed to 8465-00-926-4932 but the specification remains MIL-S-2329.

*"Sheath, Machete" (for 18 inch long, 2-1/4 inch wide blade) NSN: 8465-00-926-4932.*

# SAFETY IN TRAINING

## SAFETY IN TRAINING

Safety should be the paramount consideration during any training activity. We train so that we can protect ourselves and not get hurt. Why then would we allow being hurt in training? It is the responsibility of the instructor and all class participants to ensure the safety of all. All participants in a training activity should be led through a proper warm up and stretching routine before class begins.

## SAFETY EQUIPMENT

You should also use appropriate safety equipment for all training sessions. Equipment that should be used includes:

- Athletic Cup
- Athletic Mouth Piece
- Safety head gear
- Forearm shields
- Safety Goggles
- Safety Gloves

## SAFETY TRAINING WEAPONS

You should also use safe training weapons. A variety of training blades, bludgeons and pistols should be used from rubber to aluminum trainers. NO LIVE WEAPONS SHOULD EVER BE ALLOWED IN THE TRAINING AREA. A good friend of mine was working in a seminar with another instructor. The Instructor drew his blade and cut my friend across the inside of his forearm as part of his demo. The only problem is that he drew his live blade and not a trainer. Luckily a few stitches were all that were needed that day. I shudder to think what would have happened if the instructor would have been demonstrating a neck cut?

## OTHER CONSIDERATIONS

- Training should be conducted in reasonable proximity of emergency medical care

- Training should be conducted in a designated training area with adequate flooring, padding and ventilation.

# USE OF FORCE

## SAMPLE FORCE CONTINUUM

| ATTACKER'S ACTION | YOUR RESPONSE |
|---|---|
| Cooperation | Verbal Commands |
| Passive Resistance | Escort Control |
| Active Resistance | Control & Compliance Holds |
| Assault Which Can Result in Bodily Harm | Defensive Tactics/Mechanical Controls/Less Lethal Weapons |
| Assault Which Can Result In Serious Bodily Harm or Death | Deadly Force |

*The use of force continuum presented is a general model based on common U.S. use of force guidelines. The continuum presented is for illustrative purposes only. The reader is responsible for following all local, state and federal laws.

## FORCE CONTINUUM

The force continuum is a conceptual tool which exists to aid in determining what level of force is required and justified in controlling the actions of an attacker. Verbal commands, escort techniques, mechanical controls, and deadly force are all options which are available to a person depending upon the attacker's actions. Force escalation must cease when the attacker complies with the commands of the individual, and/or the situation is controlled by the individual. The model presented bellow consists of five levels. Physical defensive tactics are appropriate from levels three to five.

**Level One:** The attacker cooperates with your verbal commands. Physical actions are not required.

**Level Two:** The attacker is unresponsive to verbal commands. Attacker cooperation however is achieved with escort techniques.

**Level Three:** The attacker actively resists your attempts to control without being assault. Compliance and control holds as well as pain compliance techniques are appropriate actions at this time.

**Level Four:** The attacker assaults you or another person with actions which are likely to cause bodily harm. Appropriate action would include mechanical controls or defensive tactics such as stunning techniques. Impact and chemical weapons may be appropriate at this level.

**Level Five:** The attacker assaults you or another person with actions which are likely to cause serious bodily harm or death if not stopped immediately. Appropriate action could include deadly force through mechanical controls, Impact weapons or firearms. Deadly force should be considered only when all avenues for escape have been exhausted, as well as when lesser means have been exhausted, are unavailable or cannot be reasonably employed.

## DECISION OF FORCE

When making the decision to use force you should use the minimal amount of "Reasonable" force necessary to safely control the situation at hand. When using deadly force for self defense you must be prepared to articulate and justify their use of a force.

"Reasonable force" can be defined: *force that is not excessive and is the least amount of force that will permit safe control of the situation while still maintaining a level of safety for himself or herself and the public.*

*You may be justified in the use of force when they* reasonably believe it to be necessary to defend yourself or another from bodily harm and have no avenue for reasonable escape.

Escalation and de-escalation of resistance and response may occur without going through each successive level. You have the option to escalate or disengage, repeat the technique, or escalate to any level at any time. However, you will need to justify any response to resistance.

## TOTALITY OF CIRCUMSTANCES

Totality of circumstances refers to all facts and circumstances known to you at the time. The totality of circumstances includes consideration of the attacker's form of resistance, all reasonably perceived factors that may have an effect on the situation, and the response options available to you.

### SAMPLE FACTORS MAY INCLUDE THE FOLLOWING:

- Severity of the assault or battery
- Attacker is an immediate threat
- Attacker's mental or psychiatric history, if known to you
- Attacker's violent history, if known to you
- Attacker's combative skills
- Attacker's access to weapons
- Innocent bystanders who could be harmed
- Number of attacker's you are facing
- Duration of confrontation
- Attacker's size, age, weight, and physical condition
- Your size, age, weight, physical condition, and defensive tactics expertise

- Environmental factors, such as physical terrain, weather conditions, etc.

In all cases where your assessment and decision are questioned you may need to demonstrate the following:

- That you felt physically threatened by and in danger from the suspect, i.e. that the suspect's behavior (body language/ words / actions) were aggressive and threatening;

- That you used force as a last resort, and that you used the reasonable amount;

- That you stopped using force once you had the suspect and the situation under control.

- That you have exhausted all reasonable efforts to escape the situation.

# NOMENCLATURE OF THE MACHETE

There are several different models of the machete, but the basic nomenclature is the same on most of them. Besides the military type of machetes there are also various Kukri types of machetes which are also excellent for chopping brush and for self-defense.

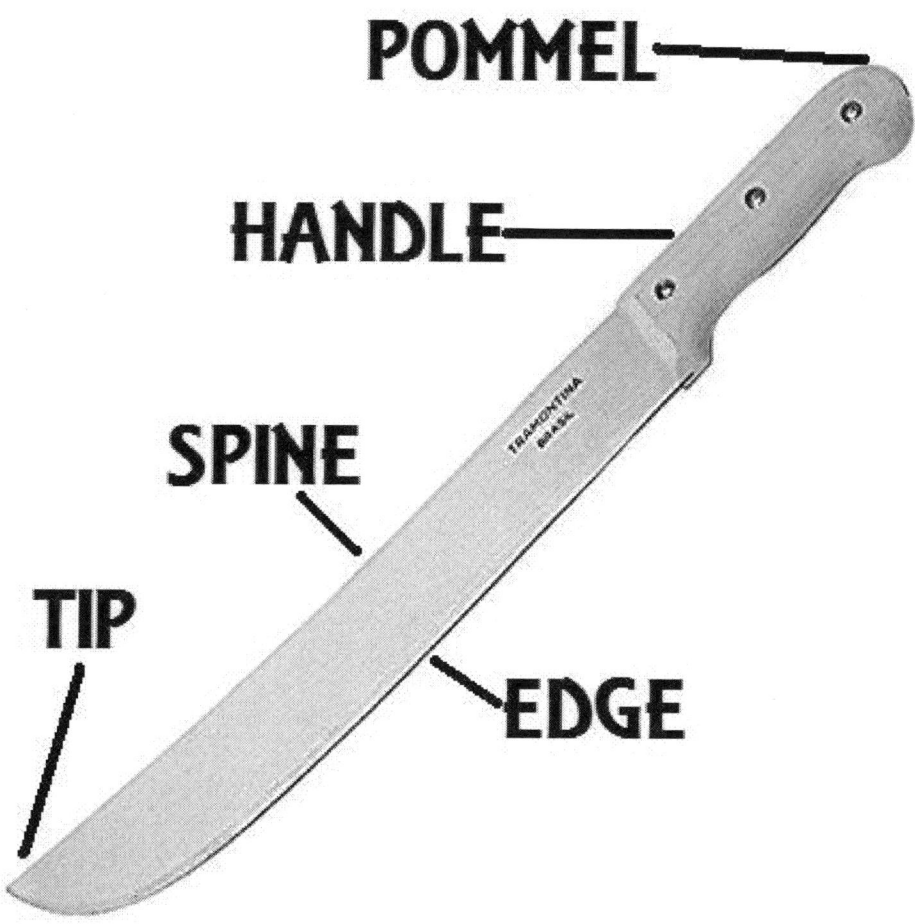

# METHODS OF CARRY

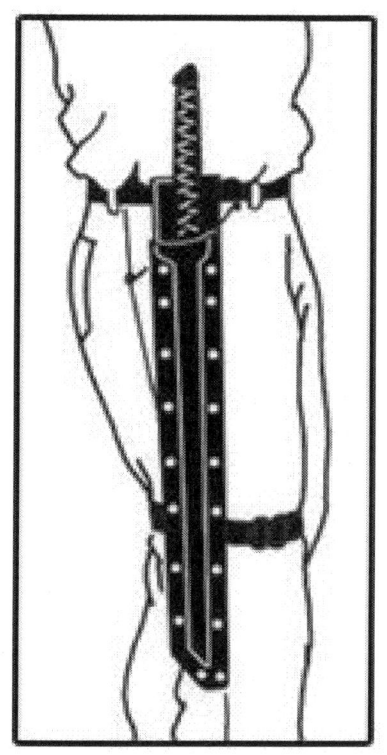

There are many ways you can carry the machete. It is important to note that the machete may not be legal to carry even though it has legitimate and practical reasons why someone may be carrying a machete on their person or in their vehicle.

You need to check with the specific laws in your area when it comes to carrying the machete. Since many states may consider the machete a knife like object and have restrictions as to blade length, you could be in trouble legally if you carry the machete.

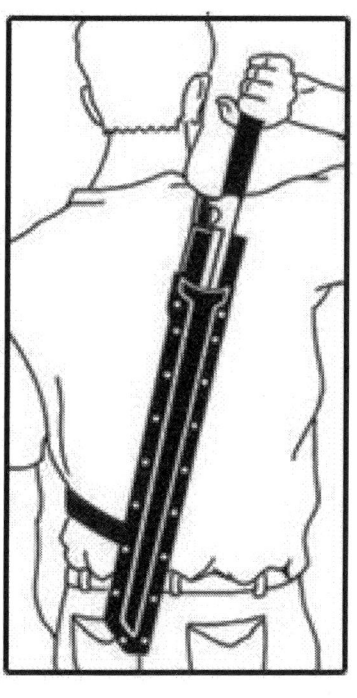

If you have a machete you should also have a sheath for it. A variety of materials are available, from common cloth sheaths, to kaidex and leather.

A Machete is normally carried on the hip. This is the most accessible carry. The machete can be worn on either side.

The machete can also be worn on the back. Or in a back pack.

# USES OF THE MACHETE

## USES OF THE MACHETE:

The machete may be one of the most common tools used all over the world. The machete is a combination type of tool in that it can be used as a knife, a small sword and an axe. It is used for a wide variety of things and the following are just a small sample of how valuable and practical the machete can be used.

1. In many countries it is used to clear brush. In fact, in the Philippines it is used for this purpose as well as for self-defense.

2. It can be used to clear trails where there is a lot of growth blocking paths.

3. Farmers use a machete to harvest a wide range of things such as oats, barley, corn, rice, sugar cane, buckwheat and other farm items.

4. The machete is also good for Chopping wood and compost

5. Trimming tree branches can also be done using a machete.

6. If you are into camping and other outdoor activities having a machete is a must have tool for a wide variety of jobs.

7. A machete is also great for fruit and nut splitting.

8. Many landscapers use a machete to clear branches, tall grass and vegetation.

9. Those living in remote areas have used the machete to ward off wild animals and snakes.

10. The machete can also be used to cut up and process meats and other types of food.

11. The machete can also be used to make traps and snares.

12. The machete is an excellent self-defense tool to be used in your home, car or outdoors in both the regular jungle and urban jungle. There are many practical uses for the machete and check on the laws in your area to determine the legal status of carrying the machete.

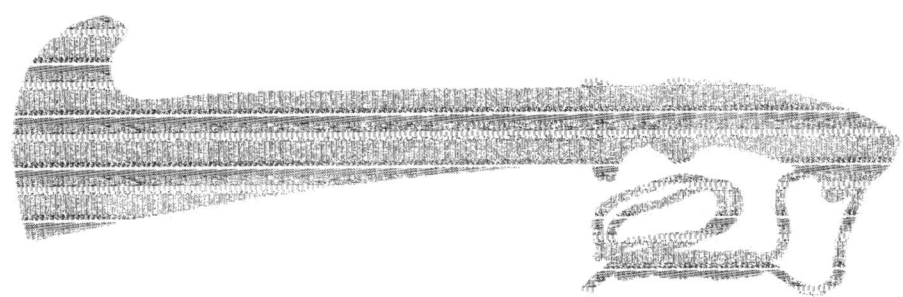

# TARGET SELECTION

## TARGETING:

You should always keep in mind that the machete is a deadly weapon and can cut through muscle and bone. It can also kill. Using the machete is using deadly force and unless you feel your life or the life of another is in danger of GREAT BODILY HARM OR DEATH, you should not use the machete. Using the machete for self-defense purposes must always be justified. You may have to explain your actions in court. Some of the situations that the court may consider your actions justified include these factors:

(1) Did the individual attacking you have a weapon and what kind of weapon did he have?

(2) Did the attacker have the means and ability to cause you great bodily harm or death.

(3) Were there multiple attackers. (4) Was there no way to escape from your attacker?

(5) Was there a way to call the police?

(6) Who started the fight?

(7) Was there no other way to avoid a physical conflict?

(8) Was there a way to handle the subject without using deadly force?

(9) Did you really feel your life was in danger? (10) Why were you carrying a machete?

Considering that using the machete is considered deadly force the following target areas should be considered if you have to protect your life or the life of another person.

1. Top of head and the sides of the head.

2. Neck area front, sides and rear.

3. Eyes.

4. Limbs such as arms, hands, and legs.

5. Sides of the body.

6. Stomach area.

7. Groin area.

8. Chest and shoulder areas

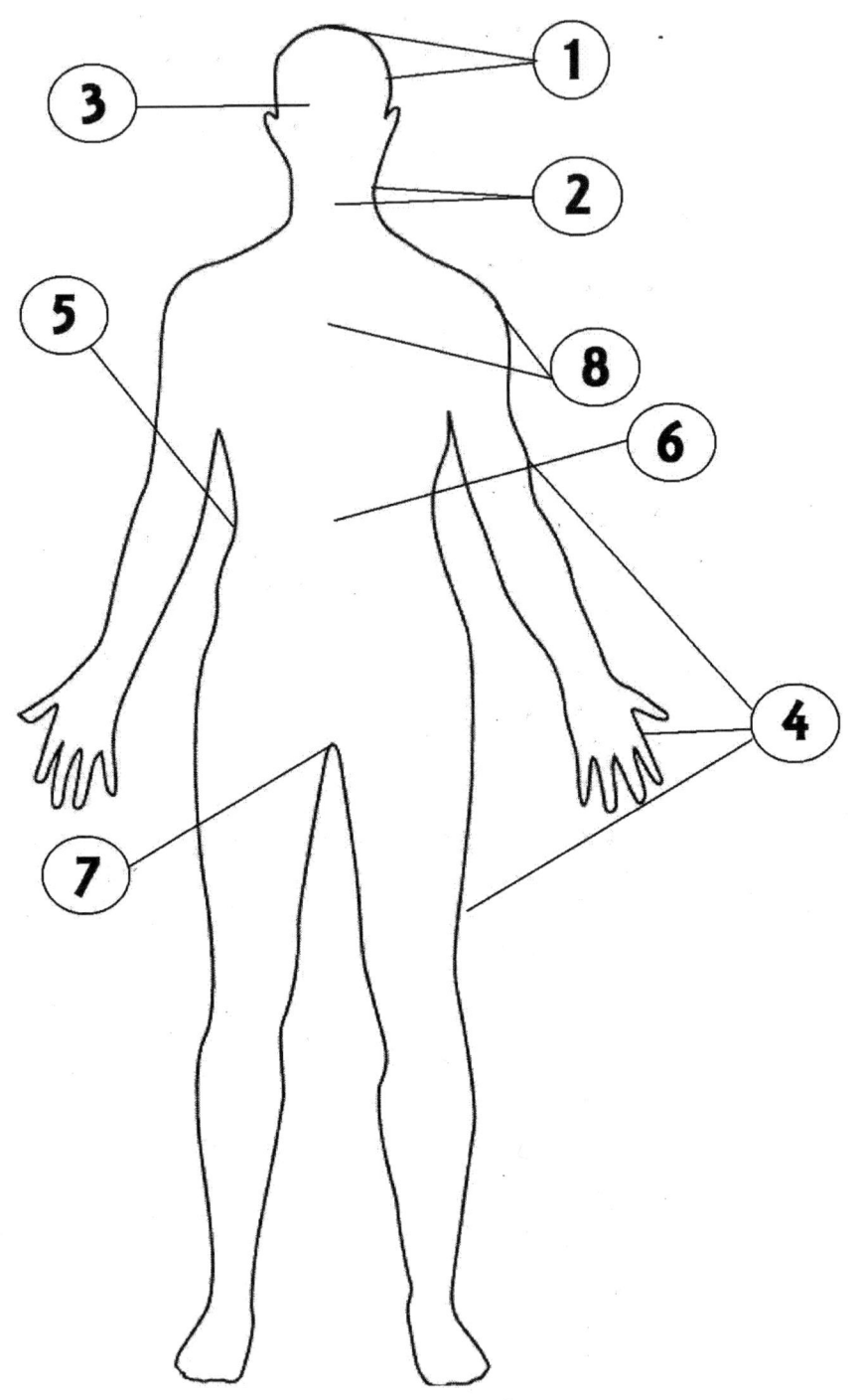

# STANCE, BALANCE

# AND

# MOVEMENT

It is essential to understand something about stance, balance and movement not just for self-defense but also for just everyday life. If you have good balance you are less likely to fall. If your movements are smooth and coordinated you can move from one position to another more easily. If your stance is strong and stable you can deliver the most power when needed. Stance, balance and movement should be as natural as possible and easy to perform.

**STANCE**

Elements of having a strong stable stance is as follows: The front leg and rear leg should be about shoulder width apart with both front and rear legs slightly bent.

## BALANCE

Balance can refer to different things but for the purposes of self-defense it means the ability to maintain equilibrium while defending yourself. By keeping the knees slightly bent with the legs shoulder width apart is one way to maintain your balance. If you have some physical problem that affects your balance you may need a support like a cane or other object to maintain your balance.

## MOVEMENT

Life is movement and in self-defense it is important to be able to move forward and back and side to side. There are many patterns of movement to help you maintain good balance and a strong stance. This manual is only going to cover four basic patterns of movement.

(1) Forward Shuffle: Begin in the basic stance position. Slide the front foot about 12 inches forward followed by the rear foot.

(2) Rear Shuffle: Begin in the basic stance position. Slide the rear foot about 12 inches to the rear followed by the front foot.

(3) Right foot side step: Move your right foot about 10 inches to the right followed by your left foot.

(4) Left foot side step: Move your left foot about 10 inches to the left side followed by your right foot.

**Note:** You should always practice these four movements with your hands up in a ready position and while the machete is in your hand as you are performing the various slashes and thrusts.

Whether you use the machete for combat with the strong side foot forward holding the machete or with your support side forward holding the machete in your strong hand is your own personal choice. Arguments can be made for both methods. In the Pro-Bushi and Pro-Systems machete course we like to practice using the machete from any stance or position we happen to be in at the time.

## THOSE WITH MEDICAL OR PHYSICAL ISSUES:

Stance, balance and movement factors are a problem for those with physical or medical issues that restrict a person from practicing standard patterns of movements. In these cases you must practice the techniques from a seated position or with a cane or other balance device. This is why some of these Machete basic techniques are also shown from a standing position and a seated position.

# BASIC GRIPPING TECHNIQUES

One of the great things about the machete is that it is easy to grip this multi-faceted tool. This manual covers four basic gripping methods when using the machete.

## ONE-HAND GRIP

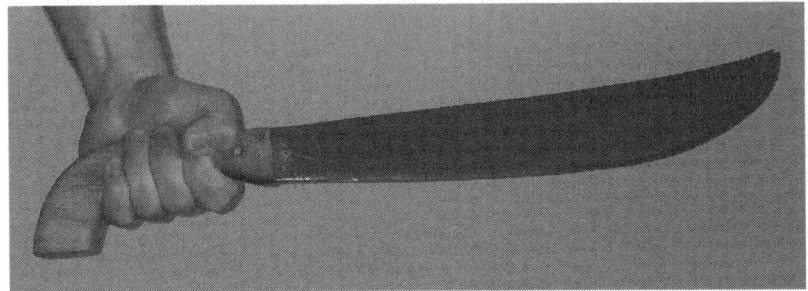

Form a fist around the grip portion of the machete and keep your wrist straight. Grip the machete firmly but not so tight that there is too much tension.

## TWO-HAND ASSISTED GRIP

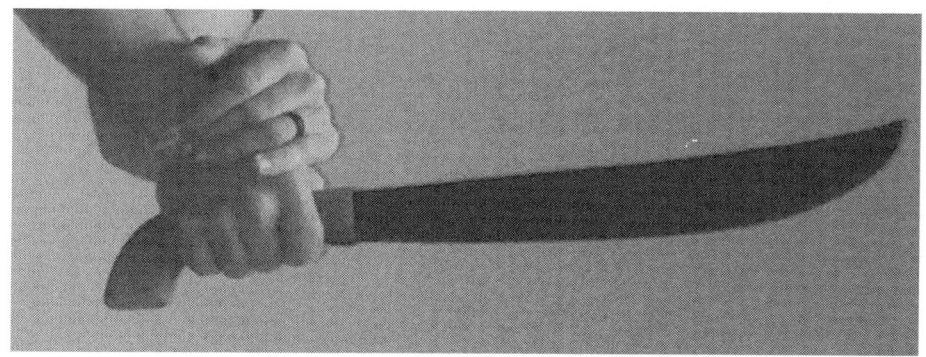

Form a fist around the grip portion of the machete and keep your wrist straight. Now place your opposite hand over your fist. NOTE: A variation is to place your opposite hand on top of your wrist to assist in your slashes and thrusts.

**ONE-HAND REVERSE GRIP**

It is important to note that using the reverse one-hand and two-hand grips are not the best ways to grip a machete; however, there may be times where you may want to experiment using the reverse grips. Form fist around the grip portion of the machete with the blade and tip pointing to the rear of your hand toward the bottom of your fist.

## TWO-HAND REVERSE GRIP

Form a fist around the grip portion of the machete with the blade and tip pointing to the rear of your body or along the forearm. Place your other hand on the wrist of the opposite hand.

# DEFENSIVE TECHNIQUES

## BLOCKING SET

This set will give you confidence in blocking and countering. Start out doing this drill slow and build up to combat speed when you have become proficient in this drill. IMPORTANT: ONLY USE A SAFETY TRAINING MACHETE WHEN DOING THIS DRILL AS WELL AS OTHER TRAINING EQUIPMENT.

## HIGH BLOCK

Holding the training machete in either the one-hand or two-hand assist, drive the machete upward over your head blocking a face or head strike.

## OUTSIDE ROOF BLOCK

To execute the outside roof block (often called a wing block) the Fighter will raise their elbow so that their weapon hand goes to the rear and the weapons tip points downward. Some choose to rest the weapon onto the arm/shoulder closest to it. The Fighter's arm and weapon should form the shape of an "A" on the outside of the fighter's body. The strike of the enemy will land on the Fighter's weapon. The Fighter should step on a 45 degree angle away from their weapon so that the enemy's strike glances instead of hitting with full force.

# LOW BLOCK

Holding the training machete either the one-hand or two-hand assist and drive the machete downward below your groin blocking a low or upward strike.

## RIGHT SIDE BLOCK

Holding the training machete in either the one-hand or two-hand assist drive the machete toward your right side blocking a strike.

## LEFT SIDE BLOCK

Holding the training machete in either the one-hand or two-hand assist drive the machete toward your left side blocking a strike.

# SLASHING TECHNIQUES

The machete is designed to slash through brush and wood. This chapter will cover the seven basic slashing techniques using the one-hand grip and the three basic slashing techniques using the reverse grip.

## OVER HEAD STRAIGHT DOWNWARD SLASH

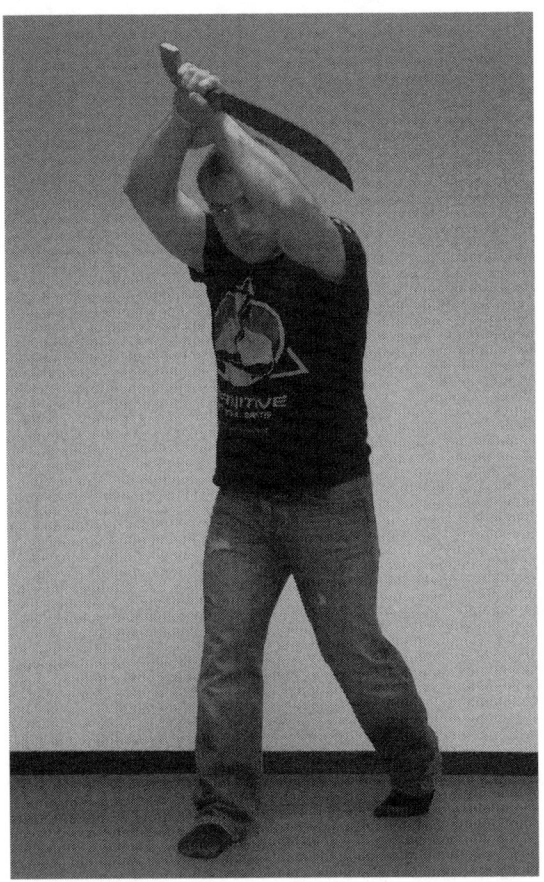

Using the one-hand grip raise the machete over your head. Come down in a straight line using not just your arms but your whole body as you slash downward.

# RIGHT SIDE 45 DEGREE ANGLE DOWNWARD SLASH

Using the one-hand grip raise the machete above your right shoulder and drive the machete downward at a 45 degree angle. Do not just use your arms but your whole body in this slashing motion.

# LEFT SIDE 45 DEGREE ANGLE DOWNWARD SLASH

Using the one-hand grip raise the machete above your left shoulder and drive the machete downward at a 45 degree angle. Do not just use your arms but your whole body in this slashing motion.

# FORWARD CROSS BODY SLASH

Using the one-hand grip swing the machete forward across your body with your palm up and the edge toward the target. Do not just use your arms but turn and twist your whole body into the technique.

## REVERSE CROSS BODY SLASH

As you finish the forward cross body slash, turn your hand palm down and swing the machete reverse across your body.

**RIGHT SIDE 45 DEGREE ANGLE UPWARD SLASH:** Using the one-hand grip swing the machete upward beginning on your right side at a 45 degree angle upward.

## LEFT SIDE 45 DEGREE ANGLE UPWARD SLASH

Using the one-hand grip swing the machete upward beginning on your left side at a 45 degree angle upward.

# FORWARD CROSS BODY SLASH USING THE REVERSE GRIP

With the palm down and the edge toward the target and using your whole body swing the machete forward across your body.   NOTE: The following photos show using a Tanto rather than a machete.

# REVERSE CROSS BODY SLASH USING THE REVERSE GRIP

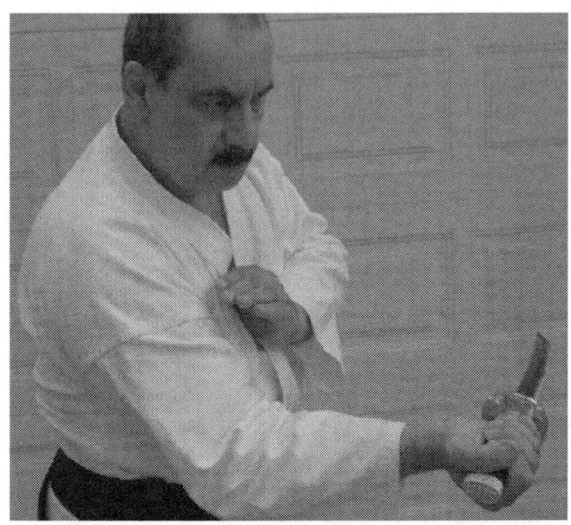

Once you complete the forward slash, with the palm down and the edge toward the target and using your whole body swing the machete reverse cross your body. NOTE: The following photos show using a Tanto rather than a machete.

**UPWARD SLASH USING THE REVERSE GRIP:** With the palm facing toward the inside of your body swing the edge portion upward from the groin area to the chest area.

**UPWARD SLASH USING THE TWO-HAND REVERSE GRIP**: Grasping the machete with two-hands and swing the edge upward. (Note: A Tanto is used rather than a machete in these photographs).

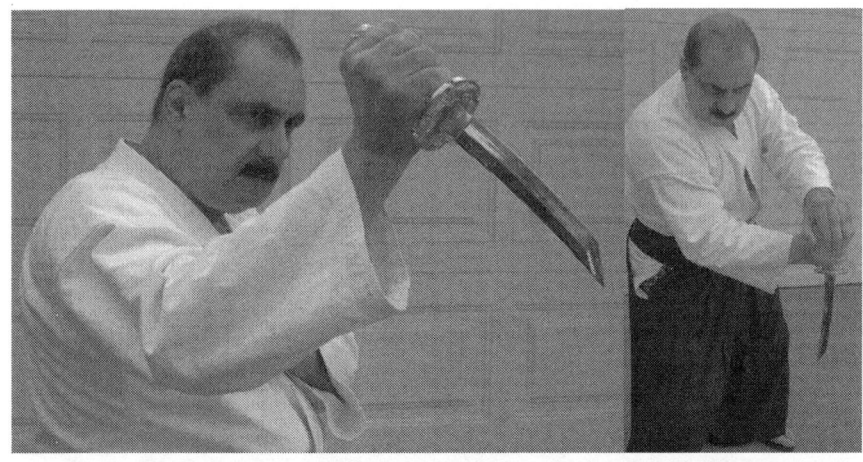

# THRUSTING TECHNIQUES

Even though the machete was designed for mostly slashing techniques; nevertheless, thrusting or stabbing techniques can also be done using the machete. This manual will cover basic thrust techniques. NOTE: In the two-handed thrusts you can either grip the machete grip portion using two hands together or by placing the assisted hand on the wrist area of your grip hand.

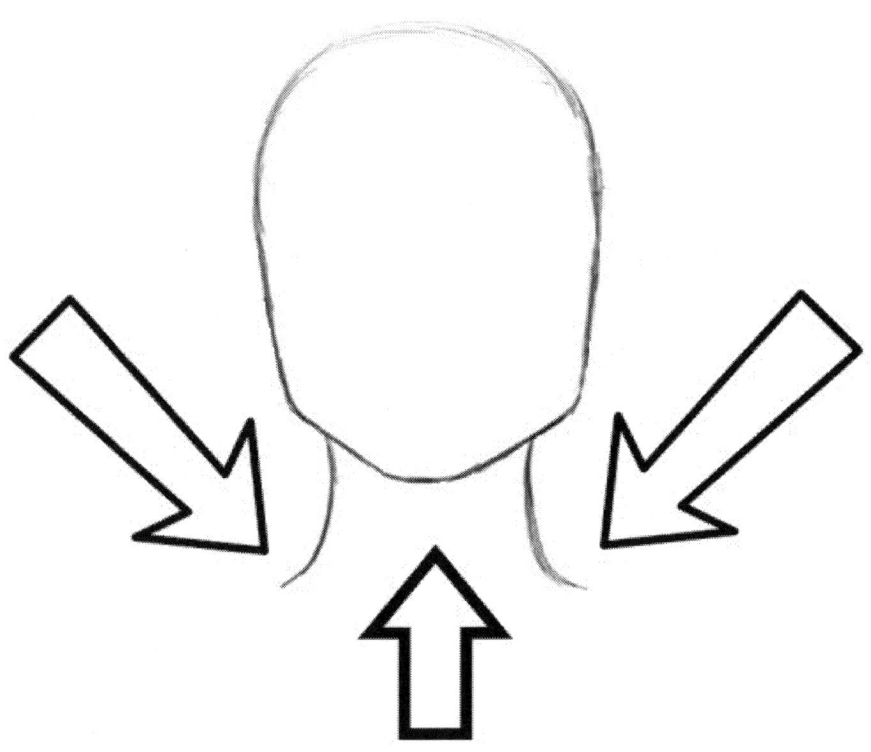

## ONE-HAND FORWARD THRUST

Using one-hand grip thrust the machete driving the tip into the neck area of the attacker. NOTE: You can perform this technique high (neck area), mid-level (rib area), and low-level (thigh area).

## TWO-HAND FORWARD THRUST:

Using the two-hand grip thrust the tip into the neck area of the attacker. NOTE: You can perform this technique high (neck area), mid-level (rib area), and low-level (thigh area). Note: Same method can be used with a Tanto.

## TWO-HAND RIGHT SIDE THRUST

Using the two-hand reverse grip thrust the tip into the neck area of the attacker. The target areas could be high, mid-level and low.

## ONE-HAND DOWNWARD THRUST

Using the one-hand or (two-hand grip) thrust the machete (or Wakizashi or Tanto) downward.

# MACHETE DRILLS

It is important to master this eight count drill using the machete. After you have mastered this drill you can add other techniques and alternate the moves to make you more skillful in the use of the machete. This eight-count drill is merely putting all the basic techniques together in flowing manner. After you are comfortable practicing these drills alone, you should use a training machete when practicing with a partner.

**THE EIGHT COUNT MACHETE DRILL:**

You should practice this drill using the one-hand grip and the two hand grip in to become proficient. . You should flow from one technique to the other using this drill. This simple drill is one of the keys to mastering not just the machete.

1. Over-head straight downward slash.

2. Right 45 degree downward angle slash.

3. Left 45 degree downward angle slash

4. Left side upward 45 degree angle slash

5. Right side upward 45 degree angle slash

6. Forward cross body slash

7. Reverse cross body slash

8. Forward thrust.

## WARM UP DRILLS:

Warm-Up drill: Your partner can use a training machete or a stick to attack you with in this drill. Slowly your partner will perform a downward strike at your head, groin, left side and right side, as you perform each block using the training machete. Do this same slow drill five to ten times.

## LEVEL ONE DRILL

As both you move around, your partner will make large moves to any of the four areas as you block the attacks. Do for one minute and change sides.

## LEVEL TWO DRILL

Back to a wall drill is done by the defender having his or her back to the wall where you cannot back up. Your partner will attack at all angles as you perform the four basic blocks. After one minute change sides.

## LEVEL THREE DRILL

Begin slowly doing this drill. Both you and your partner can now move around again with one being the attacker and one the defender. The attacker can use any attack angle and the defender must ALWAYS follow the block with a counter-attack. After one minute change sides.

## MEET THE FORCE DRILL SERIES

As the assailant Attacks the Defender, the Defender will meet the incoming attack with his weapon, coming to the inside of the opponent's arc of power. Meeting the force is most often a proactive way of addressing an incoming attack. The Defender must be aware that they use proper form, as the Defender is meeting oncoming force head on. Improper structure will buckle and give way to the enemy's attack.

## FOLLOW THE FORCE DRILL SERIES

As the assailant Attacks the Defender, the Defender is not prepared and is not quick enough to meet the incoming attack with his weapon, coming to the inside of the opponent's arc of power. The defender then uses body movement to avoid the attack and then address the attack on the "back end" by following the attack. Following the force is a most often a Reactive way of addressing an incoming attack.

## MEET THE FORCE/FOLLOW THE FORCE ADD ONS

Once the Defender has mastered these two basic drills the Defender can build upon them in the following ways. Once the Defender addresses the initial attack the Defender will adjust their position and then execute one of the following. `1

## DOWNWARD DIAGONAL CUTS

Once the Defender has addressed the initial attack, the Defender will execute forehand downward diagonal cut followed by a back hand downward diagonal cut.

## UPWARD DIAGONAL CUTS

Once the Defender has addressed the initial attack, the Defender will execute forehand upward diagonal cut followed by a back hand upward diagonal cut.

## HORIZONTAL CUTS

Once the Defender has addressed the initial attack, the Defender will execute forehand horizontal cut followed by a back hand horizontal cut.

## THRUSTING ATTACKS

Once the Defender has addressed the initial attack, the Defender will execute two thrusting attacks.

## THE CIRCLE OF DEATH

To perform this drill, multiple assailants will surround and circle the Defender. The assailants will take turns randomly attacking the Defender. The attacks will be staggered so the Defender can not time the attacks. This drill will assist the Defender in inoculating themselves to ambush or surprise attacks.

## 1-2-3 DRILL

The one 1-2-3 drill was taught to me by Reality Based Self Defense expert Jim Wagner. I learned this drill while taking Jim's Knife survival class in Buena Park California. I fell in love with the drill and I have found it to be indispensable in my training and teaching.

The drill begins with two partners, one defending and the other attacking. The attacker will make one attack and then freeze. The attacker will count a full three seconds before resetting. The attacker will feed the Defender all of the angles of attack in order and then randomly. In those three seconds the Defender can work any techniques that they like. Once this has been done a few times the team will switch to a two second count, and eventually a one second count. Now this drill has proven useful for a few reasons. First, the drill allows the Defender the opportunity to work their techniques against a variety of angles at progressively difficult time frames. Secondly, the drill is revealing. Students always work some really fancy crap when they have 3 seconds to work. By the time they get to one second they are working by necessity a much simpler and more direct skill set. Lastly the drill is an excellent way to prepare students for real time sparring. I personally do not like to let new students spar right off the bat. Newbies tend to get a little anxious or excited and they loose sight of sparring as a drill. The 1-2-3 drill allows them to work progressively towards real time sparring without neglecting the skill building along the way.

# COMBAT TECHNIQUES

The previous chapter covered some of the basic training drills to gain skill in the use of the machete in countering attacks. This chapter will expand upon what was previously covered with the focus on some of the defenses against serious life threatening attacks using the machete.

## DEFENSES AGAINST KNIFE ATTACKS

### ANGLE ONE DEFENSE

The enemy attacks the defender with a downward diagonal slash. The defender will come from behind the attacker's arm and chop down onto it. These movements in itself will most likely effect a release of the weapon due to the trauma caused to the arm. In the event that it does not, the defender will continue applying pressure, in order to clear the weapon. Once the weapon is cleared the Defender will retract their Machete, Step in and check the attacker's arm simultaneously. Once in range the Defender will forcefully chop down into the neck/head region of the attacker.

### ANGLE TWO DEFENSE

The enemy attacks the defender with a backhand diagonal slash. The defender will chop down onto the arm. This movement in itself will most likely effect a release of the weapon due to the trauma caused to the arm. In the event that it does not, the defender will continue applying pressure, in order to clear the weapon. Once the weapon is cleared the Defender will retract their Machete, Step in and check the attacker's arm simultaneously. Once in range the Defender will forcefully chop down into the neck/head region of the attacker.

## ANGLE THREE DEFENSE

The enemy attacks the defender with a horizontal slash. The defender will chop down onto the arm. The defender will continue applying pressure, in order to clear the weapon to the outside. Once the weapon is cleared the Defender will retract their Machete, Step in and check the attacker's arm simultaneously. Once in range the Defender will forcefully chop down into the neck/head region of the attacker.

## ANGLE FOUR DEFENSE

The enemy attacks the defender with a horizontal back hand slash. The defender will execute a downward block to stop the incoming blade. The defender will continue applying pressure, in order to clear the weapon to the outside. Once the weapon is cleared the Defender will retract their Machete, Step in and check the attacker's arm simultaneously. Once in range the Defender will forcefully chop down into the neck/head region of the attacker.

## ANGLE FIVE DEFENSE

The enemy attacks with a straight thrust to the abdomen. The defender will chop down onto the arm. The defender will continue applying pressure, in order to clear the weapon to the outside. Once the weapon is cleared the Defender will retract their Machete, Step in and check the attacker's arm simultaneously. Once in range the Defender will forcefully chop down into the neck/head region of the attacker.

## DEFENSES AGAINST STICK LIKE OBJECTS LIKE A BASEBALL BAT AND A TIRE IRON:

1. Attacker has a tire iron and swings it downward at your head. Use either a one-hand or two-hand assist high block combined with thrust counter using the machete.

2. Attacker has a baseball bat and swings the bat toward your left side. Use either a one-hand or two-hand assist block and counter immediately with a slash counter.

3. Attacker has a machete and swings it in a reverse cross body slash. Use either a one-hand or two-hand assist block and counter with forward slash at the attacker's neck.

4. Attacker has a sword and swings it in a 45 degree angle. Use either a one-hand or two-hand assist block and counter immediately with a reverse slash on the attacker's body.

5. Attacker has a stick and thrusts it toward your face. Use either a one-hand or two-hand assist block and counter immediately with a forward and reverse slash on the attacker's body.

# MULTIPLE ATTACKERS

If there are multiple assailants there is a chance of great bodily harm and using a machete may be justified depending on the totality of the circumstances. For example, if the two subjects are unarmed and they are smaller in size than you the court may consider using a machete excessive force; however, if the two subjects are armed with a weapon than the court may rule in your favor that you had to use the machete to defend yourself. This is why it is vital to understand the basic principles of the use of force. There must be a reasonable assumption that you are in danger of great bodily harm or death if you do not defend yourself using the machete. This is why in the following self-defense drills at least one of the attacker's has a weapon. Keep in mind that you are allowed to use only the amount of force necessary to stop further attacks, which means if you have wounded your attackers and they are no longer a threat, you must stop further physical action.

1. There are two attackers and one has a large stick: In most cases, the attacker with the weapon must be neutralized first; however, there are scenarios where this basic rule does not apply. In this case, one of the attackers has used a two-hand grab at your non-machete hand as the other attacker swings the stick at your head at the same time. The immediate danger is the stick coming down toward your head. Immediately block the stick and counter with forward slash at the stick attacker and follow through with a thrust at the attacker holding your arm.

2. There are two attackers with knives: One of the many advantages of the machete is that it is longer than most knives. With two attackers who are armed with knives you are certainly in danger of being hurt badly or killed. In this case one of the attackers is holding the knife out and is closest to you. Immediately attack the knife holding limb. The second subject closes in on you and you should immediately counter-attacks with the basic slash techniques.

3. There are three attackers with clubs: In this situation the defender has his back against a wall so no one can get behind him. As the attacker's approach the defender, the defender begins swinging his machete using all the slashes and thrusts.

4. There are four attackers armed with knives and they surround the defender: Any attempts to reason with this group are futile and the defender must immediately go into action at the first sign that one of the attacker's has entered his personal space. The defender thrusts into the closest attacker's head and slashes the second attacker's neck. The defender does a reverse slash to the attacker on the right. The fourth attacker is neutralized with an overhead downward slash.

# WARRIOR MIND-SET PRINCIPLES

In all my martial arts classes there is an emphasis on following a code of ethics. They have been handed down through word of mouth and through the written word by warrior societies since the dawn of humankind. The following ten values can serve as a basic guide for students of the martial and blade arts.

**COURTESY AND RESPECT.**

A student will show proper respect for the instructor, fellow students, and their fellow humans inside and outside the dojo. A student may be loyal and honorable in the dojo, but without following this same attitude outside the dojo, one is not living by the Code of the Samurai.

**BENEVOLENCE**

There is a saying in Japanese that you should keep in mind. "Bushi No Nasake" means "The tenderness of a warrior." There is no doubt the warrior is a dangerous person. This being the case we must temper our strength with benevolence toward our fellow man or woman. Do not mistake benevolence for weakness. Just as the warrior must be absolutely ruthless when the situation demands action, he or she must at the same time show benevolence toward those who deserve it.

**CALM AND QUIET CONFIDENCE**

The warrior should avoid any temptation to brag or boast of his/her skills and knowledge. Indeed, the most dangerous people are those who have never bragged about their skills. They showed a quiet and unassuming confidence and never demonstrated their skills until needed.

## RESTRAINT

This is a crucial component of honor. As warriors we train and harden our bodies and mind to endure the pain of battle. This being the case, we need to practice restraint in our lives. Those who are in the business of practicing the warrior arts do not look for trouble. One avoids situations that may cause us to hurt another human being. We practice restraint because we know that our skills and abilities can injure or even possibly kill an attacker. Our spirit is that of a warrior who has nothing to prove to anyone.

## LOYALTY

All warrior societies have as a central theme of "Filial duty." We owe our parents loyalty and respect. "Loyalty is the most respected virtue among warriors. Men and women of honor are loyal to their parents, superiors, and their country. Being disloyal can be one of the darkest stains on a warrior's honor." The opposite of loyalty is treachery. All warrior societies regard loyalty as a primary virtue. Those who practiced treachery in all warrior societies were scorned and dishonored.

## TRUTHFULNESS

Honesty is the virtue most talked about when it comes to honor. A dishonorable person is always to be shunned and never trusted. "The Samurai were quick to realize that honesty requires courage." They felt that lying was not just an act of immorality, but was the tool of the coward. Those who are raised in western culture and religion know the saying "The truth shall set you free." Though this can be true in many cases, the Japanese Samurai and other warriors in society view honesty in terms of courage rather than just religious morality.

## SERVICE

As warriors we hold the awesome responsibility to protect the weak and oppressed in our society. Warriors are special people and as such we must repay society for our blessings. If you are to truly live the way of the warrior than you cannot walk away from your responsibility. "You owe it to your parents, friends, coworkers, superiors, community, country, fellow students and the instructor. There are many ways to serve and we in the BUSH SATORI RYU owe it to society to help out those who need it. The Japanese call it fulfilling your "GIRI."

## OBLIGATION

At the root of all warriors honor is the principle of obligation. We are not talking about just your financial obligations, but the obligation of living in our society. Again the Japanese term "Geri" comes into play. Generally, this means the moral obligation to fulfill one's duty. This is directly related to service. "Honorable warriors look out for one another." "Geri is the glue that binds warrior societies together. However, without justice obligation can be perverted.

## JUSTICE

ustice, for the warrior, is **doing the right thing for the right reasons**. This is why criminals within any society can never have true honor. This is why obligation alone is meaningless without justice. "Remember, to be truly honorable you must always examine your obligations for JUSTICE."

## COURAGE

The average person thinks of bravery in battle when they hear or read the word courage. However, for the warrior, courage has a much deeper meaning. This means acting for the right reasons. It is not the false courage of a bully that we seek as members of BUSHI SATORI RYU, but rather the courage of a warrior with honor. Indeed, saving face is an important part of the Japanese

# REFERENCES AND RESOURCES

Use of the Monadnock Straight Baton by Joseph J. Truncale

Wakizashi-Jutsu: A Bushi Satori Ryu Basic Manual by Joseph J. Truncale

Hanbo-Jutsu: An official manual of Bushi Satori Ryu by Joseph J. Truncale

Martial Art Myths by Joseph J. Truncale

Advanced PR-24 Baton Techniques by Joseph J. Truncale

Basic Knife Handling and Knife Defense Manual by Joseph J. Truncale. Pro-Systems Publication.

Way of the Raven: Blade Combatives Volume one and Volume two by Fernan Vargas

Raven Method of Telescopic Baton by Fernan Vargas

Pro-Systems Combatives Vol. 1, 2.

Samurai Aerobics: Use of the Samurai Sword workout program by J.J. Truncale

Use of the Baseball Bat and Axe Handle for Self-Defense by J. Truncale & F. Vargas

Knife Handling and Knife Defense for Law Enforcement Officers by Joseph J. Truncale

Tanto-Jutsu: A Bushi Satori Ryu Basic Manual by Joseph J. Truncale

The Fighting Kukri: Illustrated lessons on the Gurkha combat knife by Dwight C. McLemore. NOTE: This is a must have book if you are into the Kukri machete.

Combat Machete: How to master the ultimate weapon by Jeff Anderson and Da'mon Stith DVD NOTE: This is an excellent introduction to using the machete for combat.

# ABOUT THE AUTHORS

## ABOUT JOSEPH J. TRUNCALE

Joseph J. Truncale has been a lifetime student of the martial arts, beginning with wrestling and boxing in 1956. In 1959 he joined the U.S. Navy. In 1961, he began training in Judo and Karate while stationed in Japan aboard the USS Oklahoma City. He continued his training in Judo and Karate while in the Navy until his honorable discharge in November 1963. He sought out more martial art training, joining a Shotokan Karate club, where Mr. Sugiyama, Sensei was the chief instructor.

In 1965, he joined the Glenview, Illinois Police Department and studied Judo at the Glenview Judo club at that time. He also continued his Shotokan karate training under Mr. Copland, Sensei, who was also a student of Mr. Sugiyama, Sensei. When Mr. Copland moved from the area, Mr. Truncale continued his training under Mr. Loren Rogers, Sensei, who was also a student of Mr. Sugiyama, Sensei. At that time, Mr. Truncale attended numerous law enforcement arrest and control courses, becoming a certified instructor in many police systems. He also had intense training with other Police D.T. Instructors in Krav Maga at the Illinois State Police Academy at that time. He has been involved in the martial arts for more than 40 years, studying many combat and weapon systems under numerous excellent and well-known instructors. He has earned black belts in Jujitsu ($9^{th}$ Dan USMA), Karate (Shotokan style $6^{th}$ Dan), Judo ($5^{th}$ Dan) and Kobudo (martial arts weapons). He has also studied the Yang style Tai Chi for many years with Laurie Manning, learning the 24 form, the 12 form, the Shaolin Fan form and the Tai Chi Sword form. Sifu Manning awarded him official teacher certification in tai chi.

In 1973, Mr. Truncale founded the first karate club in Glenview, teaching at the Glenview Playdium and the Glenview Park district. He also founded the first Jujitsu club at the Glenview Naval Air Station around 1980 and the first Jujitsu program at the Glencoe park district at that time.

Mr. Truncale has worked in many areas of law enforcement, but his special expertise is in police defensive tactics and police weapon fields. He has designed numerous police survival courses and has taught police and security officers from all over the world at international seminars. He is a certified International Instructor in the PR-24 Police Baton, the MEB (Monadnock Exp. Straight Baton), the Monadnock Defensive Tactics System, (MDTS), and is the Chief instructor of the Pro-Systems Mini-Baton (Persuader, Kubatons, etc.). He is also a certified Master Instructor in the CLAMP, GRASP, and OC Spray. He has had the honor to have studied under the most talented martial artists and police instructors in the world. He is the founder (Soke) of Bushi Satori Ryu, a jujitsu style that blends the traditional Samurai arts with modern combat methods. His system includes the study of 16 martial art weapons and 12 police weapons.

He has also created Samurai Aerobics, Persuader Defense System, the Mini-Baton System and Pro-Systems Practical Combatives. He has more than 2000 papers (articles, essays, reviews, poems) and more than 50 books/manuals published. He also writes several columns and has had his own newsletter called Warrior Way Reviews Newsletter. He is one of the founding directors of ASLET and has been on the advisory board of several associations such as ILEETA and IPITA. He has taught for many years at Oakton Community College and the Lattof YMCA, teaching police tactics, Jujitsu, Karate, Tai Chi, Samurai Aerobics and boxing aerobics. He has also taught numerous women's self-defense classes. He still teaches Seated Tai Chi and writes reviews on Amazon.

## ABOUT FERNAN VARGAS

Mr. Vargas holds a Bachelors of Arts from Northeastern Illinois University. Mr. Vargas also holds the designation of Violence Prevention Specialist from the National Association of Safety Professionals.

Mr. Fernan Vargas is an industry recognized trainer who specializes in Defensive Tactics, Combatives, Modern Weaponry and Combat Martial Arts. He is founder of <u>RavenTactical International</u> through which he teaches Law Enforcement Defensive Tactics. Mr. Vargas also teaches Combat Martial Arts through the <u>Military Hapkido Institute</u> and <u>Kuntao Chicago</u>.

Fernan Vargas is a current Safety Patrol Leader and Trainer for the Chicago Chapter of the Guardian Angels Safety Patrol where he has worked on several high profile anti-crime campaigns. Mr. Vargas is the founder of the official Guardian Angels Defensive Tactics System. A program used to teach Guardian Angels and the public alike. With the Guardian Angels Mr. Vargas has created <u>www.GuardianAngelsTraining.org</u> as a clearing house for training materials used by the organization. Mr. Vargas and the Guardian Angels have demonstrated the Guardian Angels Defensive Tactics System for various television stations including WGN Chicago, Telemundo, ABC Chicago, WCIU Chicago, and NBC Chicago

As a certified Law Enforcement Defensive Tactics Instructor, Mr. Vargas has taught defensive tactics to law enforcement officers at the local, state, and federal level, as well as security officers, military personnel and private citizens from around the United States and foreign nations such as Canada, Italy and Spain. Mr. Vargas has developed programs which have been approved by the Police officer training and Standards Board of several states, and adopted by agencies such as the Pentagon Force protection Agency. Additionally, organizations such as the Fraternal Order of Law Enforcement and the International Academy of Executive Protection Agents have given formal endorsements of the programs developed by Mr. Vargas and Raven Tactical International.

Mr. Vargas has been an instructor at the prestigious International Law Enforcement Educators & Trainers Association International Conference (ILEETA). Mr. Vargas has also taught at several other Leading Industry events such as the International Combatives Self Defense Association Conference, and the Saratoga Martial Arts Festival.

Mr. Vargas' has authored several books and his writings have appeared in numerous Industry periodicals such as The Martialist, Combat Warrior Magazine, Combat Survival Magazine, Muay Thaimes Magazine, Martial Arts Masters Magazine, Shinobi Nomo Magazine, The Defender, and Tae Kwon Do Times. Mr.

Vargas has also written several books including Way of the Raven Blade Combatives, and the Tactical Jujitsu Training Series.

Currently Mr. Vargas holds over twenty instructor credentials in Law Enforcement Defensive Tactics, Edged Weapons, Impact Weapons, OC Spray, Firearms, Military Combatives Combat Martial Arts, and other related disciplines. Mr. Vargas was named Trainer of the year 2011 by the Alliance of Guardian Angels and has been inducted in several halls of fame for his instruction of Defensive Tactics and Combatives. Mr. Vargas has been inducted into several Martial Arts Halls of Fame and has been awarded the Presidential Service Award and the Shinja Buke Ryu Humanitarian Award for service to the community.

# OTHER WORKS BY JOSEPH J. TRUNCALE

## Many Available at RavenTactical.com & Amazon.com

- PR-24 Police Baton Techniques: Basic and Advanced Techniques: (Co-author: with Connors Univ. of IL Press)

- Police Yawara Stick Techniques: (Co-author: with Connors Univ. of IL)

- Advanced PR-24 Baton Techniques: Monadnock Lifetime Products, Inc.

- Use of the Straight Baton: Monadnock Lifetime Products, Inc

- The Monadnock Defensive Tactics System: (Co-Author Smith) Monadnock

- The Persuader Baton(Revised original text by Eric Chambers) Monadnock

- Mechanics of Arrest and Control: For Law Enforcement. Rational Press

- The Rational Approach to Arrest and Control: Rational Press

- The Persuader Defense Systems Manual: Pro-Systems Publishing

- Basic Handbook of Hypnosis for Law Enforcement: Pro-Systems

- Rational Self-Hypnosis for Police Officers:   Pro-Systems
- Rational Self-Hypnosis for Everyone:   Pro-Systems
- Use of the Key Chain Holder for Self-Defense: (Co-author)
- The Pro-Systems Official Weapon Retention Manual: Pro-Systems
- Use of the Pepper Spray for Self-Defense Basic Manual: Pro-Systems
- The FIST(Fast-Intense-Strong-Techniques)System of Self-Defense:
- Season of the Warrior: A Poetic Tribute to Warriors:  Author House Pub.
- A Quick Course Guide to Women's Self-Defense:  Pro-Systems
- A Quick Course Guide to the Use of the Persuader Baton: Pro-Systems
- A Quick Course Guide to Total Physical Fitness:   Pro-Systems
- Use of the Scientific Method & Pseudoscience: A Quick Course Guide.
- A Quick Course Guide to Writing for Publication:   Pro-Systems

- A Quick Course Guide to Great Books of Civilization: Pro-Systems

- A Quick Course Guide to Elements of Officer Survival: Pro-Systems

- Facts and Fallacies in Police Defensive Tactics Manual: Pro-Systems

- Truth and Fiction in the Martial Arts and Self-Defense: Pro-Systems

- Common Myths about Women's Self-Defense: Pro-Systems

- A Basic Guide to Defending Against Chokes: Pro-Systems

- A Poetic Tribute to Warriors: Poems and Essay Collection: Pro-Systems

- A Tribute to Warriors: A Haiku Collection: Pro-Systems

- Nothing Ever Happens in Glenview: A Poem Collection: Pro-Systems

- The Bushi Satori Ryu Official Student and Instructor Manual: Pro-Systems

- The Bushi Satori Ryu Official 15 Weapons Basic Outline Manual: Pro-Sys

- Knife Handling and Knife Defense Manual: Pro-Systems

- Use of the Knife for Women's Self-Defense basic manual: Pro-Systems

- Basic Use of the Cane Summary Review Manual: Pro-Systems

- Basic Use of the Cane for Self-Defense Manual: Pro-Systems

- The Mighty Pen: Your Self-Defense Friend Self-Defense Manual: Pro-Systems

- The Pro-Systems 3-4 and 6-4 Basic Knife System Manual: Pro-Systems

- The Bushi Satori Ryu Official Tanto Jutsu Basic Manual: Pro-Systems

- The Revised (10 Angle System) Law Enforcement Knife Handling and Knife Defense Manual for the official course. Pro-Systems.

- The Shotokan Karate Self-Defense Manual: Practical Combat Karate.

- Karate's Multiple Strikes for Self-Defense: Karate's Forgotten Deadly Techniques: Pro-Bushi Publishing (Pro-Systems & Bushi Satori)

- The Pro-Systems and Bushi Satori Ryu Wakizashi Basic Student Manual

- Walking With Warriors: The Best of the Street Warrior.

- Never Trust a Politician: A Critical Review of Politics and Politicians Publisher E-Book Time, LLC March 2008 ISBN NO. 978-1-59824-789-3

- Baton Reverse Grip System (BRGS) Official Student Manual.

- Pro-Systems Combatives (PSC) System: Fundamentals and Principles. Official Student Manual. Pro-Bushi Publishing. ISBN Number: 978-0-9815405-1-1

- Pro-Systems Combatives (PSC) System: Advanced Techniques and Concepts Official Manual. Vol. 2. Pro-Bushi Publishing ISBN: 978-0- 9815405-0-4

- Mini-Baton Instructor Course Official Manual Pro-Systems Published in 2004.

- Martial Arts Myths: Fact and Fallacy about the Martial arts and Law Enforcement: Order from Café Press Publisher. ISBN: 1-892686-11-

- Hanbo-Jutsu: Use of the Hanbo, Cane, Walking Stick and Baton for elf-Defense. Pro-Bushi Publishing

- The Mighty Pen: Use of the Pen as a Tactical Self-Defense Tool. Pro-Bushi Publishing:

- Haiku Moments: How to write, read and enjoy Haiku. Publisher: Publish America. ISBN: 978-1-4512-9364-7

Softcover   978-1-4512-9363-0 Hardcover Order the above book from   www.publishamerica

- Predator Hunter: A Warrior's Memoir Publisher: Publish America Order from www.publishamerica  ISBN: 978-1-4560-1108-6

- Karate Combatives: Reality-Based Karate for the Street (Vol. 1)   Pro-Bushi Publishing:  ISBN: 978-0-9815405-3-5

- Weapons of Karate Combatives: Karate Combatives (Vol. 2) Pro-Bushi

- Seated Zen Karate: A Pro-Bushi Basic Manual.

- Tactical Principles of the most effective combative systems (Revising at this time).

- A Poetic Tribute to autumn: The most beautiful time of the year. (PBP)

- Haiku for special occasions (A Pro-Bushi publication)

- Short Cat Poems: A poetic tribute to cats (A Pro-Bushi publication)

- Pro-Systems Complete Straight Baton Manual for Law Enforcement and security officers Co-Author Fernan Vargas

- Use of the Axe Handle and Baseball Bat for Self-Defense by Joseph J. Truncale and Fernan Vargas

# OTHER WORKS BY FERNAN VARGAS
## Available at
## RavenTactical.com

- Way of the Raven Blade Combatives Vol. 1-8
- Way of the Raven Tomahawk Combatives Vol. 1-2
- Way of the Raven Telescopic Baton Vol. 1-2
- Cuchillo Corvo: Combat Knife of Chile
- Knuckle Duster: A Guide to Brass Knuckles
- Surviving the Active Killer
- The Great American War Club
- Native American Blade Combatives
- Things You Should know In Case I am Not Here to Tell You
- Little Dragon Dojo: Martial Arts for Kids
- Self Defense 101
- Fire Arm Defense and Retention Tactics
- The Knife Fighting of Cold Steel
- USMC Knife-Counter Knife Combatives
- It's Not A lot, It's Silat
- Rikugun Ninjutsu: Shinobi Iri and Inton Jutsu

www.RAVENTACTICAL.com

Made in the USA
Monee, IL
17 December 2025